James TILL
and Ernest
McCULLOCH

The Team That Discovered Stem Cells

SCIENTIFIC COLLABORATION

James TILL and Ernest McCULLOCH

The Team That Discovered Stem Cells

Elissa Thompson

ROSEN PUBLISHING

Published in 2021 by The Rosen Publishing Group, Inc.
29 East 21st Street, New York, NY 10010

Library of Congress Cataloging-in-Publication Data

Names: Thompson, Elissa, author.
Title: James Till and Ernest McCulloch : the team that discovered stem cells / Elissa Thompson.
Description: New York : Rosen Publishing, 2021 | Series: Scientific collaboration | Includes bibliographical references and index. | Audience: Grades 7-12.
Identifiers: LCCN 2019011187 | ISBN 9781725342293 (library bound) | ISBN 9781725342286 (pbk.)
Subjects: LCSH: Stem cells—Research—Canada—Juvenile literature. | McCulloch, Ernest A., 1926-2011—Juvenile literature. | Till, James E.—Juvenile literature. | Ontario Cancer Institute—History—Juvenile literature. | Medical research personnel—Canada—Biography—Juvenile literature. | Discoveries in science—History—Juvenile literature.
Classification: LCC QH588.S83 T4825 2021 | DDC 616.02/7740922—dc23
LC record available at https://lccn.loc.gov/2019011187

Printed in China

CPSIA Compliance Information: Batch #BSR20. For further information contact Rosen Publishing, New York, New York at 1-800-237-9932.

Find us on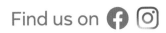

CONTENTS

Introduction

Scientific discoveries can be headline news, but they are often the result of painstaking research, many long hours of hard work, and luck. It was a combination of these factors that led the unlikely duo of James Till and Ernest McCulloch to an amazing breakthrough in stem cell research.

Most cells in the body have one job. Red blood cells carry oxygen throughout the body. White blood cells are part of the immune system. They fight viruses, bacteria, and more to keep the body healthy. Nerve cells, or neurons, transmit messages via the nervous system. Skin, or epithelial, cells provide barriers between internal cells and the environment.

But stem cells are special because they have not yet been assigned a job. Some stem cells can become any type of cell in the body. The discovery of these cells and their potential use for medical treatment had a huge impact on the world. Scientists are still working to learn more about stem cells and how to use them to treat all sorts of diseases. Many hope that stem cells can help people who have cancer or those who were born with birth defects. Some researchers are trying to use stem cells to grow new cells and tissue to replace diseased or damaged parts of

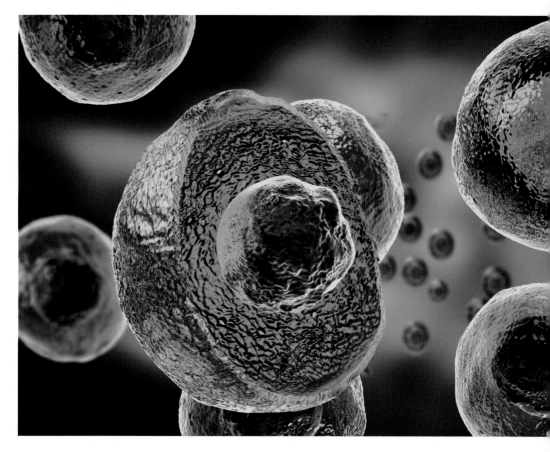

Stem cells hold a great deal of promise. Researchers continue to discover many possible ways that stem cells can help those with diseases such as diabetes and leukemia, as well as some serious injuries.

the body. There is still so much work to be done. There are so many discoveries to come.

James Till and Ernest McCulloch discovered stem cells in the 1960s. Just looking at the pair, they would have seemed mismatched. James Till was tall; Ernest McCulloch was short. They came from different backgrounds. They studied different

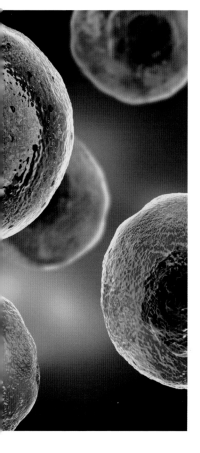

subjects. Yet when they came together, they complemented each other. Their partnership worked.

There are other examples of successful mismatched duos throughout history. Think of John Adams and Thomas Jefferson. The second and third presidents of the United States were also physically mismatched. The pair had their differences and even famously quarreled for many years. But they also bonded over shared causes and eventually mended their friendship.

The scientific world is also full of successful partnerships. Consider Marie and Pierre Curie, a husband-and-wife team who won the Nobel Prize for their pioneering work on radioactivity. They discovered the radioactive elements polonium and radium. Then there was Albert Einstein, who was credited with helping to found the field of modern physics. But it was Sir Arthur Eddington who proved Einstein's famous theory of relativity by performing an experiment during an eclipse. The two remained friends and wrote letters to each other for many years.

Working with a partner can lead to success that might not have been found alone. By pairing up, one has access to different viewpoints, varied ideas, and independent experiences. Science is all about uncovering the mysteries of the universe step by step. Alongside a partner, achieving scientific success can feel much more possible. Ernest McCulloch and James Till are great examples of how teamwork can lead to an incredible scientific discovery.

CHAPTER ONE

How It All Began

How does one grow into an accomplished scientist? Is there a certain type of degree to earn? A school one must attend? Ernest McCulloch and James Till had childhoods that were very different. They both went to college for different reasons, during a time when fewer people pursued higher education. And yet, in the end, they ended up in the same place at the same time.

Bun's Early Childhood

Ernest McCulloch was born in Toronto, Canada, on April 27, 1926. As an infant, he earned the nickname "Bun," given to him from his grandmother. People called him Bun or Bunny all his life, whether he liked it or not. "I can't shake it," McCulloch said of his nickname. "People that I meet, I'd give my proper name to and for years they use my proper name. And then they run into somebody from Toronto and it all gets lost."[1]

McCulloch's family was wealthy. They had a home in Toronto and a lake cottage, where he learned to sail in the summer. His father was a doctor, but at first McCulloch was not sure he would follow in his father's footsteps. Like many young children,

Ernest McCulloch is pictured here in New York City at the ceremony for the 2005 Lasker Award for Basic Medical Research on September 23, 2005.

McCulloch dreamed of different careers. He was going to be a pilot or a police officer. He eventually decided to become a doctor, "for a very foolish reason. It struck me that the great advantage of being a doctor was that you were your own boss, and I liked that idea."[2]

After graduating from the private high school Upper Canada College, he attended medical school at the University of Toronto and graduated with honors in 1948.[3] While studying at the Lister Institute in London, McCulloch began to consider devoting his life to research, instead of practicing medicine.

McCulloch returned to Canada and worked at a hospital, while performing research as well. He coauthored a paper on

Canada's Great Depression

On October 29, 1929, the New York Stock Exchange suffered a dramatic loss. The United States, Canada, and many other countries around the world entered a Great Depression. Nearly 30 percent of people were out of work. Twenty percent of Canadians got money and food from the government, which eventually had trouble gathering enough resources for all its citizens.[4] Farmers were among the occupations hardest hit. The price of wheat was very low. A major drought and dust storms plagued the farms and made it hard for crops to grow. This is the world James Till was born into in 1931.

The Great Depression lasted for ten years in Canada, and some called the decade "the Dirty Thirties." The country began to recover economically when World War II was under way. Men who were still unemployed enlisted in the army as a way to earn wages.

kidney circulation in rabbits in 1952, which was published in the *British Journal of Surgery*. In 1957, he was offered the head of hematology position at the Ontario Cancer Institute. It was a fateful decision that would lead him to become a scientific pioneer. But his career move away from practicing medicine was not without controversy in his personal life. Some of his family

During the Great Depression, many people were desperate for work. Men traveled far from home to search for opportunities to make money for their families.

members disapproved of him becoming a research scientist. Medical doctors can earn more money than researchers.

"Everybody has their criteria for success," McCulloch said. "Mine wasn't money."[5]

James as a Boy

James Till was born on August 25, 1931, in Lloydminster, Saskatchewan, Canada. His parents were homesteaders, or farmers. Even as Till went on to great success, he continued to return to the farm to help with the harvest.

Till had a few simple reasons for continuing his education past high school. One was that he wanted to see if he could do it.

The other? His parents insisted. He wound up following his brother to the University of Saskatchewan, selecting the school over the University of Alberta because they offered him a fifty-dollar entrance scholarship. "Fifty dollars seemed like an awful lot to me at that time," Till recalled.[6]

The scholarships kept coming, and so Till continued his education. He eventually went on to earn his doctorate degree in biophysics at Yale University in the United States. The stress of his education did not bother

James Till is pictured here in New York City on September 23, 2005, where he and McCulloch received the 2005 Lasker Award for Basic Medical Research.

him too much because, as he said, "I knew I could always go back to the farm."[7]

Eventually, Till wanted to return to Canada. Because he wished to leave the United States, he turned down an offer from Yale to be an assistant professor.[8] He searched for a position, and eventually his postdoctoral work brought him back to Canada. Later, he was recruited by Dr. Harold Johns (1915–1998), head of the Physics Division at the Ontario Cancer Institute.

The Ontario Cancer Institute

The place where Till and McCulloch would meet and embark on their remarkable research was called the Ontario Cancer Institute (OCI). It was the first hospital to be dedicated to cancer in all of Canada. The research center opened in 1957, and the hospital opened to patients in 1958. However, it turned out that people did not like getting treated at a place with "Cancer" in the title, so the hospital portion of the building was renamed Princess Margaret Hospital.[9]

Till and McCulloch began work at OCI when it opened. The philosophy of the place encouraged researchers to reach their goals. Till and McCulloch collaborator Louis Siminovitch (1920–) played a key role in establishing the OCI.

"We were able to nurture new students, new trainees, new staff people that built up a repertoire of scientists who are spread right across the country, and some of them in the states," Siminovitch said.[10] "I had a very simple plan. I was not going to just hire scientists; I planned to hire leaders. We started out like a ball of fire—with good people, first-rate research and excellent programs." Siminovitch was known for recruiting more than twenty-five exceptional scientists for the Ontario Cancer Institute over the years.[11]

OCI's Princess Margaret Hospital in Ontario, Canada, still performs important cancer research today. Many exciting medical discoveries have been made at the institute over the years, including McCulloch and Till's groundbreaking work.

Everyone at OCI worked hard to succeed, and many important discoveries were made at the facility over the years. As the center opened, scientist Vera Peters (1911–1993) was already known for her groundbreaking work treating those diagnosed with early Hodgkin disease with high-dose radiation. Then, in the early 1980s, researcher Tak Mak (1946–) discovered the T-cell receptor. This breakthrough had a great effect on the field of immunology.

By the twenty-fifth anniversary of the OCI's opening, the hospital was seeing more than double the anticipated number of patients.[12] Research, and the equipment required to do the work, was also changing and growing in size. This all meant that the OCI was rapidly running out of space. Eventually, it was decided that a new hospital would be built. By the mid-1990s, researchers had moved into a new building to continue their work, which still stands today.

The Ontario Cancer Institute was an exciting, collaborative place for Till and McCulloch to work. Soon, they would make history together.

CHAPTER TWO

An Unlikely Pair

Scientific research can involve a great deal of creativity. One must look at problems in different ways and consider many outcomes. What better way to dream of inventive solutions than with someone different from you by your side? This is what happened to McCulloch and Till. Their differences contributed to their eventual success.

Opposites Attract

Many who worked with McCulloch and Till comment on how unalike they were in both their appearance and personality. Till was thin, and nearly a head taller than the stocky McCulloch. Till was always neatly dressed—not true for McCulloch, who was often more rumpled. "Clothes did not matter to Dr. McCulloch, and his clothes were often covered with chalk, which he often held in his mouth, ready to draw diagrams on a blackboard to push an idea to the extreme to see where it would take you," said Alan Bernstein (1947–), who worked with the duo and is now president and CEO of the Canadian Institute for Advanced Research.[1] McCulloch liked the theater and movies, and a conversation with him could go in many

Their differences helped them thrive. McCulloch, at left, was an out-of-the-box thinker and doctor. Till, at right, was a linear-minded physicist. Their partnership began in the 1960s, and they remained friends for decades.

different directions. Till was more reserved and favored straight-forward explanations.[2] Their differences wound up greatly complementing each other.

The Fated Partnership

So how did a biophysicist and a doctor come to work together? When McCulloch and Till began working at OCI, their different disciplines kept them apart. They saw each other occasionally, as OCI held evening mixers where scientists could learn about others' research, but they did not collaborate. It was a rule by Dr. Johns that led them to a partnership that would last for many years.

McCulloch was beginning an experiment in which he would use radiation on laboratory mice to prepare them for bone marrow transplantation. Dr. Johns had established a guideline at OCI that only physicists could use radiation. And so, Till volunteered to help.

Johns was well known as a mentor and teacher. He encouraged a great many students during his career, so it is not surprising he was the driving factor in pairing up Till and McCulloch. "Johns was a team player," said his son-in-law Dr. Clive L. Greenstock, "and believed that if a thing was worth doing, it was worth doing to the best of one's ability. He was a great teacher and a hard worker who brought out the best in those around him."[3]

Till and McCulloch got along immediately, respecting each other's ideas and work. "We talked on equal terms," Till said, with neither scientist taking the lead.[4] McCulloch did not take charge. He began collaborating with Till in a respectful and fair manner right away. "We knew that when we disagreed, that the answer was something different," McCulloch said, "We had different approaches, but they were complementary."[5]

Harold Johns, pictured here in 1980, created a life-saving cancer treatment that is still used today to help those in need. He also encouraged scientific collaborations, such as the one between Till and McCulloch.

Dr. Harold Johns and Cobalt-60

The scientist responsible for pairing up Till and McCulloch was also a famous research pioneer. In 1951, Johns and his team created cobalt-60 therapy in Canada. It was an innovative way to treat cancer. The treatment enabled radiation to reach tumors deep inside the body, which the lower-level X-rays used at the time could not access. The therapy saved millions of people suffering from cervical, bladder, and prostate cancer. Some estimate that the therapy has helped more than seventy million people since it first came into use.[6] The first patient treated with the therapy lived into her nineties! Cobalt-60 therapy is still used in some underdeveloped countries because it is simple and effective.[7]

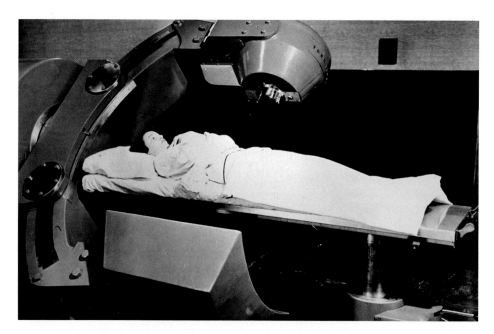

Harold Johns's cobalt-60 treatment allowed many patients to live long lives after being diagnosed with cancer.

In many ways, the disciplines the men had studied contributed to their different ways of looking at the research. Physics is an area of study based in math and numbers, favoring Till's straight-line, quantitative way of thinking. Medicine and biology favored McCulloch's thought process. "He reveled in thinking big about ideas and encouraged speculation," said his former colleague Bernstein.[8]

A Mistake Grows Camaraderie

The duo began preliminary work on McCulloch's research. But during one of their early experiments, Till was surprised by the mice's behavior. He closely checked his calculations and realized he had made a mistake! He had incorrectly calculated the radiation doses. Till knew he had to say something, so he went directly to McCulloch to talk. He said in an interview:

> So I very shamefacedly went to Ernest McCulloch and I said, "I made a mistake, the right dosages are such and such" … and I expected that that would be a sort of disruptive effect on our collaboration, well, it wasn't a collaboration yet. And it was quite the opposite. I think Ernest McCulloch was first very pleased that I told him about the error immediately and secondly I think he was delighted that a physicist could make a mistake! You know, these physicists always project the image that they're infallible. So that broke the ice. And in fact it made it feasible, I think, for us to be very frank with each other … in terms of discussing what experiments we wanted to do, and anything else under the sun that came to our minds. And that persisted.[9]

By being honest, Till won McCulloch's admiration, which allowed the pair to begin working together more closely and in a more balanced manner.

Why Radiation Mattered

In August 1945, the United States detonated two atomic bombs over the Japanese cities of Hiroshima and Nagasaki. More than eighty thousand people were killed immediately, with many more dying from radiation poisoning later. Scientists had been working to create this powerful new weapon, but there was still much to learn about its effects.

In the following years, the public's concerns about the effects of radiation helped with Till's research. People were scared about another bomb being dropped and what would happen to those exposed to radiation. They wanted to know if there was a treatment to heal people once exposed to such dangerous chemicals.

The mushroom clouds from the two atomic bombs dropped on Hiroshima (*left*) and Nagasaki (*right*) shoot up into the sky. These devastating blasts killed thousands of people and sickened many others.

"There was much concern about the threat of nuclear weapons, that we might have to fight an atomic war," Till said. "So, being able to ameliorate the effects of total body irradiation by having a bank of marrow was a big deal. Some of our very early funds came from the Defence Research Board of Canada. They were very interested in this when other agencies were less excited. I still feel a debt of gratitude to that agency."[10] This money helped Till and McCulloch perform their research.

Scientists Working Together

Till and McCulloch were successful in part because they came from different areas of study. They could think critically about problems in distinct ways. This is called interdisciplinary research. When people come from different areas of study, it can help researchers be more innovative and try more imaginative solutions.

At the Ontario Cancer Institute where Till and McCulloch worked, students had to take at least one course in a subject area other than what they had studied in college. So physics students had to take a biology course, and vice versa.[11] This helped bring researchers together to develop new ideas. This type of approach can work for many modern problems too. By thinking beyond what one knows, the possibilities are endless.

The Discovery

The stage was set. Till had agreed to help McCulloch with the radiation in his experiment. It was time to get to work.

The Experiment

The scientists set about performing the experiment. Till and McCulloch began by giving the mice large doses of radiation. Thanks to previous trials, they knew how much radiation to use to kill the correct number of the mice's cells. The mice were eight to twelve weeks old. The scientists put them into groups of twenty-five, made up of approximately half male and half female mice.[1] Then, the day after the radiation, the mice were injected with a small number of marrow cells. Till and McCulloch used a much smaller amount of marrow cells than was being used in other experiments at the time.

The mice were kept in cages in small groups of three to four and fed. They were observed for ten to eleven days. Some died during this time. The surviving mice were killed after ten to eleven days, so Till and McCulloch could take out and examine their spleens. The scientists discovered that the spleens of the mice had lumps. The lumps were larger in the mice that had lived eleven days after the experiment.[2]

Till and McCulloch used laboratory mice throughout their experiments. First, they exposed the mice to radiation. Then they injected them with marrow cells to see how the mice responded. What they found changed the world.

One fateful Sunday afternoon in 1960, McCulloch decided to try counting the lumps on the mice spleens. And thus he made his big discovery. The number of lumps had a linear, or directly proportional, relationship to the number of marrow cells injected.[3] For roughly every ten thousand marrow cells injected, there was one nodule, or lump.[4] This meant that the number of lumps was directly related to the number of marrow cells injected. But why?

Blood cells

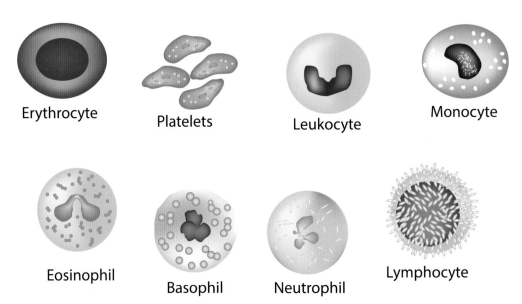

Erythrocyte

Platelets

Leukocyte

Monocyte

Eosinophil

Basophil

Neutrophil

Lymphocyte

Bone marrow produces different types of blood cells that perform various tasks throughout the body. Erythrocytes, or red blood cells, deliver oxygen, while white blood cells, such as leukocytes and lymphocytes, fight infection.

Till and McCulloch called the lumps "colonies" of cells. And inside the colonies were different types of cells! There were red blood cells, white blood cells, neutrophils, and lymphocytes. This meant that the one type of marrow cell injected had created all those other cells. This was big news. The scientists were excited. They had discovered an entirely new theory of how blood was made.[5] And, if the scientists thought further, it could mean exciting new things about how tissue and even organs were grown.

The Publication

In the scientific community, researchers communicate their discoveries by publishing their findings in peer-reviewed journals. This was Till and McCulloch's next step after making their extraordinary findings. In 1961, they published an article in *Radiation Research* titled "A Direct Measurement of the Radiation Sensitivity of Normal Mouse Bone Marrow Cells."

Interestingly, the duo had agreed, in a show of their collaborative partnership, to reverse the order of their names each time they were published. For peer-reviewed papers, the person whose name is first is often considered the lead researcher, on whom more accolades are bestowed. But the pair didn't think much about that. As Till has said, the pair didn't want any fuss over who was going to take credit for the work.[6] McCulloch's name had gone first on a 1960 paper in *Radiation Research*, "The Radiation Sensitivity of Normal Mouse Bone Marrow Cells, Determined by Quantitative Marrow Transplantation into Irradiated Mice." This meant Till was the first author on the famous 1961 paper. And so, throughout history, they were known as Till and McCulloch.

At first, their paper did not get much of a response from the scientific community. According to Till, scientists were not yet focused on stem cells; they were still thinking about the recent discovery of the double-helix structure of DNA by James Watson, Francis Crick, Rosalind Franklin, and Maurice Wilkins. Another reason their discovery didn't make such a big splash was that *Radiation Research* did not have a very big audience.[7] In addition, the duo did not use the term "stem cell" in their work. Instead, they referred to them as "colonies of proliferating cells." But a lack of immediate recognition didn't stop Till and McCulloch. They kept at their work.

Science in the 1960s

There were a lot of exciting scientific discoveries happening in the 1960s.[8] In biology, scientists discovered mammography, which helps to detect tumors in breasts. They also completed the first heart transplant. Work in bone marrow transplants was also progressing, which would relate to McCulloch and Till's work.

It was also a very exciting time for space travel, as countries raced to see who could make it to the stars and beyond first. In 1966, astronauts from the Soviet Union landed an aircraft on the moon. Then, in 1969, American astronauts Buzz Aldrin (1930–) and Neil Armstrong (1930–2012) walked on the moon. People across the world watched on their televisions as the astronauts planted an American flag on the moon.

More Research: Tracing Origin

Till and McCulloch continued on with their research. They began working with another scientist, Andrew Becker (1935–2015). Becker was a doctor who was also interested in research, like McCulloch. He came to work with the duo as Till's doctoral student. He helped the pair to further examine their extraordinary findings. He was tasked with discovering how many cells from the injection were required to create a spleen colony.[9]

To trace the bone marrow cells that started the spleen colonies, Becker used chromosomal markers. The markers could trace the original cell that came from the injection. It would show which cells from the injection regenerated in the mouse's body and where, because those new cells would also contain the marker. Becker looked at a great deal of cells: forty-two

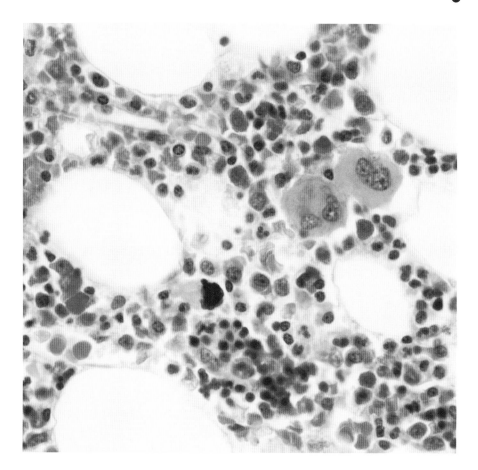

Bone marrow cells, like those pictured here, create platelets as well as red and white blood cells. An important cornerstone of Till and McCulloch's work, bone marrow cells were also the focus of transplant research in the 1960s.

spleen colonies in thirty-six animals. Four colonies had cells with marked chromosomes. And nearly all of the cells in those colonies contained the chromosomal marker.[10]

The marked cell colonies were made up of red blood cells, white blood cells (or leukocytes), and platelets. All of those different cell types had come from a single bone marrow cell injected into the mice! Till and McCulloch had discovered hematopoietic stem cells, or stem cells that created different types of blood cells.[11]

In 1963, McCulloch and Till, along with Becker, published another article, this time in the popular scientific journal *Nature*. "Cytological Demonstration of the Clonal Nature of Spleen Colonies Derived from Transplanted Mouse Marrow Cells" showed that the colonies full of different cells formed in the mice's spleens came from one cell.

Next Steps: Proving Replication

There was still more research to be done. Next, Till and McCulloch wanted to see if the spleen colonies could renew themselves, or make new, additional colonies. To do this, they worked with fellow Ontario Cancer Institute researcher Louis Siminovitch. First, they separated out spleen colonies into their different cell types. Then, they prepared a set of mice and administered radiation. The mice were injected with cells from a specific colony. These mice also developed colonies, proving the cells could replicate.[12] The men published their findings, "The Distribution of Colony-Forming Cells Among Spleen Colonies," in the *Journal of Cellular Physiology* in 1963.

Defining the Term "Stem Cell"

The term "stem cell" began appearing in scientific literature as early as 1868. German biologist Ernst Haeckel (1834–1919), who greatly supported the theory of evolution from Charles Darwin, used the phrase to describe a one-celled organism evolving into a multicellular organism.[13] Scientists began working further with the concept, examining how fertilized eggs turned into embryos, and the cells that helped with that transition.

Ernst Haeckel was one of the first scientists to use the term "stem cell." Haeckel used "stem cell" to describe a process in evolution, and the definition has changed over the years.

Some credit geneticist Edmund B. Wilson (1856–1939) with defining the term "stem cells" in his 1896 book, *The Cell in Development and Inheritance*.[14] Many scientists were inspired by that publication, and the concept of stem cells grew, though researchers still had not solidified their idea.

It wasn't until Till and McCulloch began counting those spleen colonies that the wonder of stem cells truly began to come into focus. Through their work with Becker and Siminovitch, Till and McCulloch were able to develop their own stem cell definition. "We outlined a functional definition of stem cells: that they must be capable of self-renewal, that they must be capable of giving rise to differentiated descendants, and that they must be capable of extensive proliferation," Till recalled. "That was actually the first functional definition of stem cells, and we had to invent it, because there wasn't one that we could use."[15]

The Reaction

An important part of the scientific world is that when a team publishes a paper on their research, other scientists need to be able to replicate the work in their own laboratories. This helps prove that what one has accomplished is true, and that the results are indeed correct.

At first, some scientists had trouble replicating Till and McCulloch's experiments. In one instance, the mice kept dying before day ten. This meant there was not enough time for the spleen colonies to grow. But Till and McCulloch believed in their work.[16] Till simply told the other scientists to begin by using healthier mice. If the mice were healthier before radiation, they were more likely to survive until day eleven, which was when the spleen colonies became truly pronounced.

Still others were not convinced by Till and McCulloch's research. Their discovery was considered controversial by some.

One scientist, John Trentin (1918–2005), proposed an alternative hypothesis. He believed that the cells in the colony formed based on what their neighboring cells were becoming. Scientists backed the different hypotheses; even some working at the Ontario Cancer Institute favored Trentin's research over their coworkers'. "I didn't take it personally. It was a professional disagreement. I figured it would sort itself out," Till said.[17] Eventually, Till and McCulloch's hypothesis became the more accepted explanation. The field of stem cells was growing, thanks in part to their discovery.

CHAPTER FOUR

A Quiet Victory

What happens after someone makes a world-altering scientific discovery? Does the scientist become very famous? Well, sometimes. The names of Isaac Newton, Stephen Hawking, and Charles Darwin are familiar to many people. But others are not, such as Ada Lovelace (1815– 1852), who helped found the world of computer science. Or Abbie E. C. Lathrop (1868–1918), who bred the kind of laboratory mice that many scientists still use in research today. Till and McCulloch are among these, the recognized but not famous. They may not be well known, but they did change the world.

Reception

The scientific community began to accept Till and McCulloch's discovery of hematopoietic stem cells. Their experiments were eventually able to be replicated, and their discoveries have stood the test of time. Their 1961 and 1963 articles have been cited many times as other scientists do further research. But for the most part, Till and McCulloch's lives did not change. They continued their research at the Ontario Cancer Institute without much fuss. "Both James and I are private people," McCulloch said. "We do not seek celebrity."[1] Decades went by before the men received some accolades.

The Lasker Prize

In 2005, forty-four years after their findings were published in *Radiation Research*, the pair was awarded the Lasker Prize. They were heralded as "the fathers of stem cell research." The Lasker Prize is very celebrated. It is considered by many to be the United States' most prestigious medical prize and is sometimes called "America's Nobel." It came with a $50,000 prize that the pair split.[2]

When the pair won the award, other scientists took time to celebrate the duo's achievement. In an article published in *Cell*, Saul J. Sharkis (1944–2016), a longtime professor of oncology at the Johns Hopkins University School of Medicine, wrote of their legacy:

> When new students join my lab, I insist that they set up a spleen colony assay. The assay teaches techniques such as intravenous injection and sterile handling of bone marrow cells. It also

Mary Lasker, shown here in 1957, cofounded the Lasker Foundation. The organization promotes and advocates for medical research. Each year, the Lasker Awards recognize important researchers and scientists for their work.

shows reproducibly the clonal nature of stem cells as the students carry out the same cell dose-response curve for injected bone marrow cells that McCulloch and Till used to so elegantly show that the number of spleen colonies is directly proportional to the number of bone marrow cells injected. I can think of no more deserving a team for the Lasker award than that of Earnest [*sic*] McCulloch and James Till, whose revolutionary studies ignited the field of stem cell biology so many years ago.[3]

Till and McCulloch were pleased with their award, though McCulloch said he wished it had happened a decade or so earlier, when his legs were stronger, so he could truly enjoy the experience.[4] So why did the award take more than four decades? Dr. Joseph L. Goldstein (1940–), chairman of the Lasker jury in 2005, helped select winners. He explained that sometimes older research was awarded much later because it can take time to appreciate a discovery's significance. With the benefit of time and perspective, along with a great deal of blossoming excitement about stem cell research, Till and McCulloch's discovery could be better celebrated.[5]

Till and McCulloch themselves asked "Why now?" in an article, "Perspectives on the Properties of Stem Cells," in *Nature Medicine* in 2005. They cited multiple reasons for their late-breaking award, including the innovative research happening in the early 2000s. But overall, they acknowledged that, thanks to hindsight, they knew they had helped kick-start research on both adult and embryonic stem cells.

Ever humble, the pair wrote, "We weren't deliberately seeking such cells, but, thanks to a felicitous observation originally made by McCulloch, we did stumble upon them. Our experience provides yet another case study of both the value of fundamental research and the importance of serendipity in scientific research."[6]

At the award ceremony, Till expressed surprise that their work was still of such interest: "I … remember how exciting it was to see the first evidence of what turned out to be multipotent stem cells of the blood-forming system," he said during his acceptance

A researcher works with embryonic stem cells at the Burnham Institute in California. Scientists believe that stem cells are an important part of the future of medicine, with many mysteries waiting to be unlocked.

The Canadian Medical Hall of Fame

In 2004, Till and McCulloch were inducted into the Canadian Medical Hall of Fame. Located in Ontario, where the duo did their ground-breaking research, the hall honors medical heroes. "Their contribution was profound and influenced the growth of their fields—in fact they established a whole field of inquiry that is beginning to be recognized as containing the keys to [an] eventual cancer cure," said Dr. Norman Iscove, a professor of medical biophysics at the University of Toronto.[7]

For this honor, the longevity and relevance of their discovery was also praised. "Their work gains a new freshness with the current interest in harnessing the developmental program of stem cells for therapeutic purposes," the hall noted.[8]

speech. "We knew at the time that we had become involved in something very interesting. But we definitely didn't anticipate that our work might continue to be of some interest so many years later."[9]

The Politics of the Nobel Prize

Many consider the Nobel Prize the most prestigious award in the world. While this may be up for debate, there's no doubt winning the Nobel comes with a large cash prize—of almost $1 million! Some say that winning the Lasker Prize is an indicator that one will win a Nobel Prize. And while there is evidence to that effect, as many Lasker winners have gone on to win a Nobel, this is not always the case.

The selection of Nobel Prize winners is subjective, and it can also be political. The nomination process has several phases. Certain people, who are deemed qualified, make nominations

Rosalind Franklin was one of four scientists who revealed the structure of DNA. She died in 1958, four years before the three men she worked with won the Nobel Prize for the discovery.

each year. Then, a small committee selects the final short list of candidates from those compiled nominations. Finally, the Nobel Assembly votes on winners in the different categories, including physics, chemistry, physiology or medicine, and more. Much of the process is very secretive, and the Nobel committee does not comment publicly on any of it. They also keep their nomination list secret for fifty years.

There have been many controversies surrounding the Nobels over the years, as some have won the prize while others were snubbed. For example, though Francis Crick, James Watson, Maurice Wilkins, and Rosalind Franklin are known as the quartet of scientists who discovered the double-helix structure of DNA, only Crick, Watson, and Wilkins won the Nobel. Franklin had died four

years prior to the Nobel being awarded in 1962. But unsealed nomination documents showed she was not even nominated. The Nobel committee will only allow the nomination of three people per achievement.

From left to right: Professor Maurice H. Wilkins, Dr. Max Perutz, Dr. Francis Crick, author John Steinbeck, Professor James D. Watson, and Dr. John Kendrew pose with their Nobel Prize diplomas in Stockholm, Sweden, in 1962.

Till and McCulloch never made it to the Nobel white-tie award ceremony in Sweden. Colleagues of the pair have said they nominated the duo for the award several times, to no avail.[10] Why didn't their discovery warrant the award? Perhaps it was that their first paper in 1961 was not published in a well-known journal. Perhaps it is because they did not start off using the term "stem cell" in their articles. Perhaps the committee found other discoveries more deserving. No one can know for sure.

Till and McCulloch were scientists who cared greatly about their work and each other. And, as both have said, it wasn't about the awards for them. It was about the science.

CHAPTER FIVE

Moving Forward

What does a person do after making a huge scientific discovery, no matter the reception? For Till and McCulloch there was only one thing to do: get back to work!

Other Research: Pioneering the Bone Marrow Transplant

Till and McCulloch's research did much to explain the functions of bone marrow. Scientists at the time were beginning research on how to perform bone marrow transplants. That is when a healthy person gives some of his or her bone marrow to someone whose bone marrow is no longer working correctly, often because of a disease such as cancer. McCulloch believed it was obvious bone marrow transplants would be a useful medical procedure because bone marrow is damaged during both radiation and chemotherapy, two common cancer treatments.

The collaborative nature of OCI also extended to the attached Princess Margaret Hospital. McCulloch made an attempt at bone marrow transplantation early in OCI's existence. He worked with pediatrician John Darte (1920–1975) from the children's

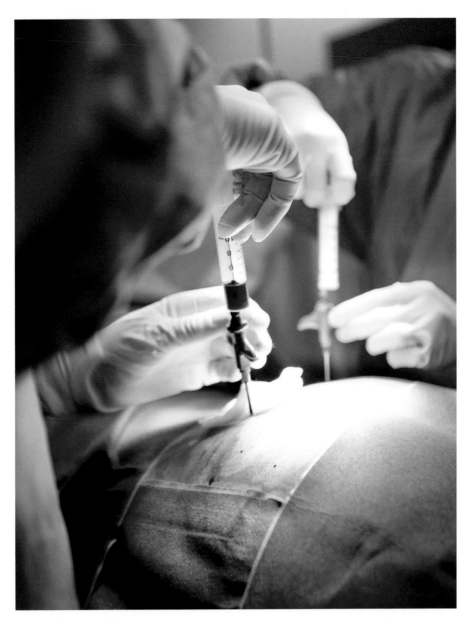

Doctors retrieve bone marrow from a patient during a surgical procedure. Bone marrow transplants can save the lives of patients suffering from leukemia and other blood disorders and cancers.

cancer ward. Together, the men performed three bone marrow transplants on children with leukemia.[1] Only one child reached a temporary remission. Discouraged by the results, the pair did not continue the experiments. Darte moved on from the OCI for some time, though he eventually returned to briefly become director of the institute in the mid-1970s before his sudden death. McCulloch and Darte did not publish their findings in any scientific journals and only discussed the results at a meeting.

A particular problem for bone marrow transplants was that laboratory tests of the procedure using animals did not successfully predict how the human body would behave during the transplant. As McCulloch noted, many bone marrow experiments, such as his and Till's, were done using inbred mice. McCulloch wrote, "Transplants between mice of the same strain are successful, since genetically identical cells are not seen as foreign."[2] When a bone marrow transplant was attempted with humans—who were not identical twins—the body reacted to the transplanted cells as if they were foreign cells to be attacked.

Others were also working on bone marrow transplants around the world. E. Donnall Thomas (1920–2012) was researching in the United States, experimenting with bone marrow transplants between dogs. Then, in 1969, Thomas was successful. He completed the first human sibling-to-sibling bone marrow transplant.[3] He eventually went on to complete a bone marrow transplant using an unrelated donor eight years later. This accomplishment led to the creation of the bone marrow registry. For his research, he won the Nobel Prize. Today, there are millions of people signed up to be potential donors. This helps those in need of a bone marrow transplant to potentially match with strangers who are compatible.

McCulloch was not the scientist to complete the first bone marrow transplant. But the work he and Till did in establishing

E. Donnall Thomas (*right*) stands next to Leland Hartwell. Both won the Nobel Prize for Medicine: Thomas in 1990 and Hartwell in 2001. Thomas's research led to successful bone marrow transplants and the creation of the bone marrow registry.

how bone marrow functions, and the intricacies of blood cell growth and regeneration, helped inform the scientific world as it worked toward other discoveries.

Teamwork and Mentoring

Teamwork was always very important to Till and McCulloch, from the very beginning as they joined forces. They valued each other's background, education, and input. But their enthusiasm for teamwork did not stop with their own collaboration. Over the years, the pair worked with and encouraged many other scientists. There were Andrew Becker and Louis Siminovitch, with whom they worked on their momentous discovery—and shared first authorship on their groundbreaking papers. In the years after 1963, a great many other scientists came through Till and McCulloch's lab. There, they learned about the exciting world of stem cells—and the importance of partnership.

Till and McCulloch's willingness to mentor students meant that the impact of their research lasted long beyond their 1960s groundbreaking studies. Today, there are scientists all over Canada and around the world who spent time in their lab and came away better for it. Alan

Bernstein worked with the men at OCI. Bernstein went on to help found the Canadian Institutes of Health Research and helped greatly increase research funding for the country. Then there is Dr. Robert A. Phillips, who was president and CEO of the Ontario Cancer Research Network.[4] He has also worked hard to expand cancer research. Dr. Connie Eaves (1944–) worked with Till and McCulloch. She is now a professor of medical genetics at the University of British Columbia and a distinguished scientist at the Terry Fox Laboratory.[5] She researches leukemia stem cells.

Dr. Alan Bernstein worked with Till and McCulloch before going on to forge his own important career. Here he is pictured discussing Canadian guidelines for stem cell usage at a 2002 press conference.

These scientists are doing their own important work to help make the world a better place.

The Next Generation

Till and McCulloch's network has only grown over the years. The love of mentorship they instilled in their mentees has been passed on to a new generation of scientists. These scientists favor collaboration over competition, says Dr. John Dick (1954–), a coleader of acute leukemia research at the Ontario Institute of Cancer Research. Dick also works with cancer and stem cells. Bernstein and Phillips—former students of Till and McCulloch— both mentored Dick. Dick said of Till, McCulloch, and other early leaders at OCI:

> They did science in its purity and with openness. They imbued that in their trainees, so that we're now living by the principles that they set down 40 years ago in terms of how we operate and how we function … People would rather collaborate than compete. That creates a very open atmosphere. It means students can easily move from one lab to another. They can get information—nobody's holding on to information tightly because they're worried that someone's going to scoop their latest data. When you can talk about your latest idea before you've done any experiments, that creates a legacy that is enormous.[6]

Fellowship was an important part of OCI. It was also a way of life that Till and McCulloch would continue to practice at their laboratory throughout their careers.

Canada and Stem Cell Research

One important way that the OCI contributed to the research landscape in the 1960s and today was that it brought many important scientists to work in Canada. Till and Siminovitch

Louis Siminovitch: Founding Father of Genetics

Like Till, OCI colleague Louis Siminovitch studied abroad but returned home to spend his career in Canada. "He could have gone to many countries in the world," Dr. J. C. Laidlaw (1921–2015), a well-known Canadian endocrinologist, said of Siminovitch. "Canadians like him decided to stay in Canada and make their contributions there."[7] While at OCI, Siminovitch did a great deal of research that some say laid the groundwork for many genetic breakthroughs still happening today. During his five-decade career, he published nearly two hundred scientific papers. But his most enduring legacy may be his mentorship. Like Till and McCulloch, he valued teamwork and helping others to achieve their research goals. "So many people go back in their histories to an experience with Lou that was a changing point that really made their career," said Dr. John Evans (1929–2015), founding dean of the McMaster University Medical School.[8] The collaborative nature of OCI didn't help just Till and McCulloch, but many other scientists as well.

searched for jobs after finishing their education. They wished to return home to Canada, and having the OCI, a top research facility, in Ontario helped them to do just that. In turn, they helped to make Canada into a research destination.

This is still true today. Dr. Connie Eaves, who worked with Till and McCulloch, went on to work in British Colombia. She said

Louis Siminovitch was another scientist at the Ontario Cancer Institute who made great contributions to the medical world. He also encouraged partnerships among the scientists and was a champion for Canada's research community.

when she first moved to British Colombia, it was like "being on the frontier." She called it "a place where you can develop new things," which was "very attractive to scientists who wanted to explore new areas."[9] This has helped bring even more talented scientists to the country throughout the years.

Having Canada as a research destination is especially impressive because of its large geographic area but relatively small population. Dr. Michael Rudnicki, scientific director of the Stem Cell Network, credits the pioneering and collaborative spirit of Till and McCulloch with jump-starting this effort across the country.[10]

Till and McCulloch had a lasting effect on the field of stem cells and their country, both through their own work and through their mentorships of others.

CHAPTER SIX

What's Next for Stem Cells

Decades after Till and McCulloch first found the spleen lumps that would lead them to discover stem cells, the field of stem cell research continues to grow and change. A hot-button political issue, stem cell research has a great deal of potential to treat diseases, including heart disease and cancer. It also comes with a fair amount of controversy.

Stem Cell Creation

Scientists sometimes prefer to use embryonic stem cells in their research because they can turn into many different types of cells and tissues, while other types of stem cells are more limited in their developmental potential. An embryo must be able to change into all sorts of cells to create a baby. Meanwhile, the stem cells Till and McCulloch discovered can only become different types of blood cells.

In 2007, Japanese scientist Shinya Yamanaka (1962–) made an exciting discovery. He created cells that acted like embryonic cells, even though they were not.[1] Yamanaka found that by

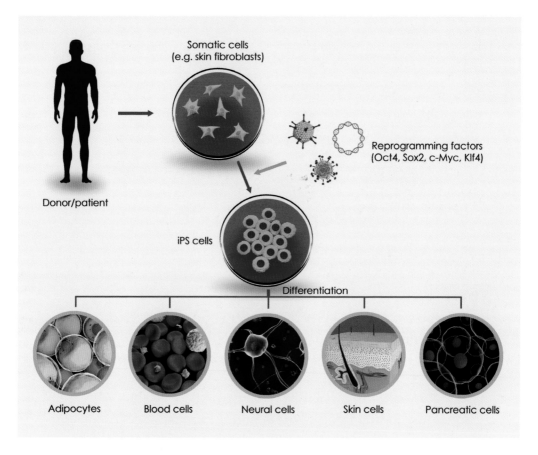

An induced pluripotent stem cell begins with a somatic cell, which can be reprogrammed to behave like an embryonic stem cell. This cell can then take many different forms.

altering the genes of certain adult cells, the cells can change to look and act like embryonic stem cells. Called induced pluripotent stem cells (iPSC), these cells enable scientists to keep working on stem cell research while politicians debate the ethics of using embryonic stem cells. For his discovery, Yamanaka won the Nobel Prize. Many scientists are now using iPS cells to develop new therapies to treat diseases.

Stem Cell Controversies

Researchers believe that stem cells may hold the cure to many diseases. So why would anyone want to limit scientists' work or stop them from experimenting with stem cells? It is because of where the cells come from.

The stem cells Till and McCulloch discovered were hematopoietic. They came from bone marrow and produced different types of blood cells. But many researchers work with human embryonic stem cells, which come from an embryo, a fertilized egg in the early developmental stages. Some people are opposed to this research because it requires destroying the embryo. Antiabortion activists in particular oppose stem cell research because of this.

In 2001, President George W. Bush put limits on the money the government could spend on stem cell research. He said the government would only fund research on sixty already established embryonic stem cell lines. This meant that no more embryos would be destroyed. But many scientists found this rule too limiting.[2]

Then, in 2009, President Barack Obama relaxed the rules Bush had put in place. He signed an executive order that said federally funded researchers could use embryos no longer needed from fertility clinics. Those embryos had to have been created without government money. But President Donald Trump revisited the issue of all fetal tissue use during his time in office, putting the fate of such research into question.

Stem Cell Solutions

So how can stem cells help people who are sick? There are still a lot of unanswered questions, but many believe there is a great deal of hope as well.

Types of Stem Cells

There are several different types of stem cells, in addition to hematopoietic stem cells that create different types of blood cells, which Till and McCulloch discovered.[3]

Embryonic Stem Cell: An undifferentiated cell from an embryo. These stem cells can develop into many different cells and tissues.

Adult Stem Cell (or Somatic Stem Cell): An undifferentiated cell found in muscle and tissue. These cells can renew themselves and also change into different types of cells found within the muscles and tissue where they originated, helping with renewal and repair.

Bone Marrow Stromal Stem Cells (or Mesenchymal Stem Cells): Located in bone marrow, these stem cells can make bone, cartilage, and fat cells.

Neural Stem Cell: Residing in the brain, these cells can become neurons as well as some types of non-neuronal cells.

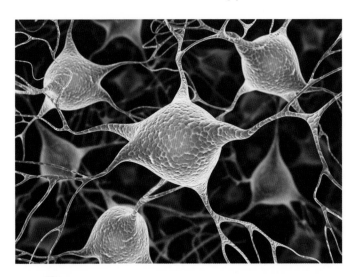

Neurons
send signals
throughout the
body via the
nervous system.

Drug Testing

Before a new type of medication can be released onto the market for people to use, it must go through many different tests and trials to make sure it is safe. Often, these tests are performed on animals. Animal rights activists oppose this because they feel it is cruel to animals. It can also be difficult because, as McCulloch learned when attempting bone marrow transplants, laboratory mice do not always behave as a human body would. Some scientists have begun using stem cells to test drugs, especially the toxicity of drugs. By using stem cells, researchers can more accurately predict the drug's effect on a human and refrain from unnecessarily using laboratory animals.[4]

Stem Cell Transplant

Many decades ago, McCulloch attempted three bone marrow transplants, but he did not have success. Today, thanks in part to his and Till's discovery, stem cell transplants can help save the lives of cancer patients.

The procedure is in some ways similar to what Till and McCulloch did to the mice in the early 1960s. Large doses of radiation and chemotherapy are used to kill all cancer and bone marrow stem cells in a sick person's body. Then, stem cells are reintroduced. Depending on the type of transplant the patient is undergoing, which relates to the type of cancer being treated and other factors, the stem cells have different origins. In an autologous stem cell transplant, the patient receives his or her own previously harvested stem cells. Sometimes, these cells are further treated to try to ensure that the patient does not get cancer again. In an allogenic stem cell transplant, the new stem cells come from a donor.[5] Sometimes this donor is a family member. But the donor can also be unrelated, such as someone found through a registry. These transplants can save people's lives.

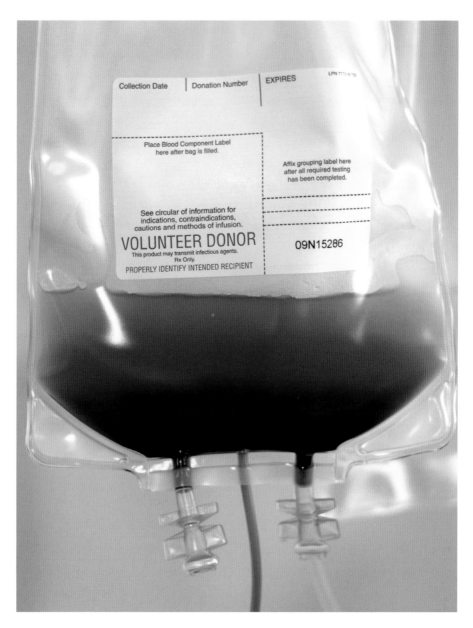

Stem cells can come from many different sources, including one's own body. Pictured here are a donor's stem cells, which could potentially be used in a transplant for another person or perhaps for the donor him or herself at a later date.

Cell-Based Therapies

Perhaps someday, someone in need of a new heart will not have to wait for an organ donation. As it works now, an organ donation must match the person's blood type and more. It must also be quickly available. There are so many variables to consider, all of which can jeopardize an already ill person's health. What if stem cells could fix the problem by growing new tissue? This is something scientists are working on; it is called stem cell–based therapy.

Scientists are investigating different types of stem cells, including embryonic, cardiac, iPS cells, and more, that can help with cardiovascular disease. Cardiovascular disease, which includes heart attacks and strokes, is a top cause of death each year. Some trials have been performed on mice and pigs as scientists try to regrow damaged tissue. There have also been a few instances of studies on humans. In these cases, a person was injected with stem cells during open-heart surgery. Sometimes, the stem cells helped improve circulation or helped damaged tissue. This experiment is controversial and there is still a great deal of research to be done. But scientists hope for promising results in the future.[6]

Diabetes is another disease that many hope stem cells can help with. Diabetes is a disease that affects a person's blood sugar. With type 1 diabetes, a person's body does not make insulin, a hormone created in the pancreas that helps control blood sugar levels. Researchers are working to develop stem cell therapies that will get a diabetic person's pancreas to make insulin when needed.[7]

Another ailment researchers have been working to treat with stem cells for many years is Parkinson's disease. Parkinson's disease increasingly affects a person's movements, sometimes

TYPES OF DIABETES

Diabetes is a disease that affects how a person's body makes or uses insulin. Some hope that stem cells will cure diabetes.

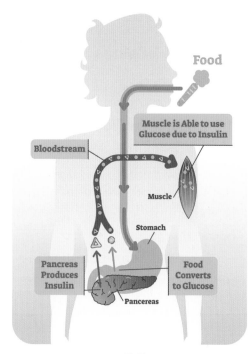

Healthy

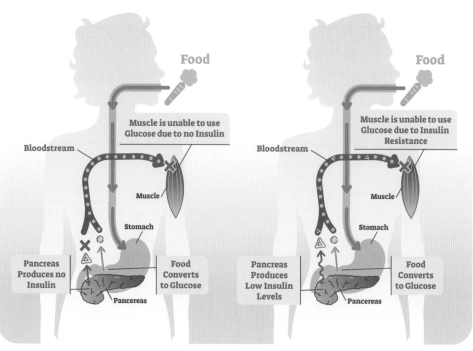

Type 1

Type 2

causing tremors or even stiffness. Researchers are working to restore brain cells damaged by the disease with stem cells.

There is so much exciting work happening in the world of stem cells, as scientists try to help those suffering from disease. Though there is still research to be done, Till and McCulloch's discovery set the stage for many potentially incredible therapies.

Conclusion

Scientific discoveries take time, hard work, and luck. For James Till and Ernest McCulloch, it was a combination of all three factors that led them to discover stem cells. When speaking about their discovery many years after the fact, McCulloch was, as always, humble. "It came about, as so often happens, as an incidental result of an experiment done for completely different reasons," he said.[1] But that "incidental result" would change the scientific world for decades to come.

The journey their lives took, from different childhoods in Canada to scientific pioneers, was an exciting and sometimes surprising one for the pair. After all, as a child, McCulloch wasn't sure he wanted to be a doctor like his father. Meanwhile, Till often considered going back to the family farm to work. Yet they became dedicated scientists who excelled at their areas of research. They complemented each other, and together, they made each other's work better. They were meticulous in their research, thanks to Till's background in physics and his dedication to quantitative results. And it was McCulloch's amazing ability to brainstorm, and his willingness to think beyond the big picture, that led him to count the bumps on the spleen that fateful Sunday in 1960.

James Till and Ernest McCulloch remained close friends until McCulloch's death in 2011.

Till has likened their 1960s discovery as similar to winning the scientific lottery. And so, while Till and McCulloch may not have ever become household names, as a pair they changed the research world. They are hailed as the fathers of stem cell research. They started science on an amazing road of discovery.

Their partnership and willingness to share credit and knowledge led to another impressive legacy. The network of scientists they built up during their decades of work at the Ontario Cancer Institute has gone on to do and discover exciting things, with even more to come. Their mentees have expanded the world of Canadian scientific research, and the funding needed to grow even further.

The world of stem cells is brimming with potential, even as it is dogged by controversy. Some say a cure for diabetes or even cancer may be within reach thanks to stem cells. No one is sure what the future will bring. But many researchers are confident that stem cells have much to offer the field of biology, medicine, and the world.

For Till and McCulloch, their equal and enduring partnership was a large part of what made all their success possible. The pair spent more than five decades together. And their names will be linked in history books for years to come.

Upon being inducted into the Canadian Medical Hall of Fame in 2004, Till said of his friend, "It's a delight to be with him, to come into the hall of fame at the same time, because our names have been linked together so much and for so long, it's nice to be together."[2]

Together, they made each other better. Together, they made history.

CHRONOLOGY

- **1896** Edmund B. Wilson uses the term "stem cell" in his famous text *The Cell in Development and Inheritance*.
- **1924** Ernest McCulloch is born in Toronto on April 27.
- **1931** James Till is born on August 25 in Saskatchewan, Canada.
- **1945** The United States detonates atomic bombs over Hiroshima and Nagasaki in Japan, killing more than eighty thousand people immediately and sickening thousands more from radiation.
- **1948** McCulloch graduates from the University of Toronto medical school with honors.
- **1952** McCulloch publishes one of his first research papers in the *British Journal of Surgery*.
- **1953** James Watson, Francis Crick, Rosalind Franklin, and Maurice Wilkins discover the double-helix structure of DNA.
- **1954** Till begins studying at Yale University.
- **1957** The Ontario Cancer Institute opens, and researchers start their work; Princess Margaret Hospital opens a year later.
- **1960** McCulloch and Till discover the linear relationship between marrow cells and cell colonies and publish their paper "The Radiation Sensitivity of Normal Mouse Bone Marrow Cells, Determined by Quantitative Marrow Transplantation into Irradiated Mice," in the academic journal *Radiation Research*.
- **1961** McCulloch and Till publish their paper "A Direct Measurement of the Radiation Sensitivity of Normal Mouse Bone Marrow Cells" in *Radiation Research*.
- **1963** McCulloch, Till, and Andrew Becker publish a paper in popular journal *Nature* on their research, "Cytological Demonstration of the Clonal Nature of Spleen Colonies Derived from Transplanted Mouse Marrow Cells."

- **1969** E. Donnall Thomas completes the first bone marrow transplant using a sibling donor.
- **2001** President George W. Bush limits US embryonic stem cell research to certain already established strains.
- **2004** McCulloch and Till are inducted into the Canadian Medical Hall of Fame.
- **2005** McCulloch and Till win the prestigious Lasker Award for their research breakthrough.
- **2007** Shinya Yamanaka creates iPSCs (induced pluripotent stem cells).
- **2009** President Barack Obama lifts some embryonic stem cell research restrictions in the United States.
- **2011** McCulloch dies on January 19 at age eighty-four.
- **2019** President Donald Trump's administration begins looking into fetal tissue use in research.

CHAPTER NOTES

Chapter One ❋ How It All Began

1. Joe Sornberger, *Dreams & Due Diligence: Till and McCulloch's Stem Cell Discovery and Legacy* (Toronto, Canada: University of Toronto Press, 2011), p. 22.
2. cdnmedhall, "Dr. James Till-Dr. Ernest McCulloch Canadian Medical Hall of Fame Laureate," YouTube, January 6, 2011, https://www.youtube.com/watch?v=P7N-fUKjT-s&feature=player_embedded.
3. Lawrence K. Altman, "Ernest McCulloch, Crucial Figure in Stem Cell Research, Dies at 84," *New York Times*, February 1, 2011, https://www.nytimes.com/2011/02/01/health/research/01mcculloch.html.
4. "The Great Depression," Canadian Museum of History, updated April 21, 2010, https://www.historymuseum.ca/cmc/exhibitions/hist/medicare/medic-2c01e.html.
5. Sornberger, p. 26.
6. cdnmedhall, "Dr. James Till-Dr. Ernest McCulloch."
7. Joe Sornberger, "T.O. Stem Cell Pioneers Win 'America's Nobel,'" *Toronto Star,* September 18, 2005.
8. Sornberger, *Dreams & Due Diligence,* p. 25.
9. Ernest A. McCulloch, *The Ontario Cancer Institute: Successes and Reverses at Sherbourne Street* (Montreal, Canada: McGill-Queen University Press, 2003), p. 7.
10. cdnmedhall, "Dr. Louis Siminovitch," YouTube, January 11, 2010, https://www.youtube.com/watch?v=izukkcPGLEY.
11. "Mount Sinai's Dr. Lou Siminovitch Appointed to the Order of Ontario," University of Toronto Faculty of Medicine, February 1, 2012, http://www.mshri.on.ca/?page=1912.
12. McCulloch, p. 141.

Chapter Two ❋ An Unlikely Pair

1. Lawrence K. Altman, "Ernest McCulloch, Crucial Figure in Stem Cell Research, Dies at 84," *New York Times*, February 1, 2011, https://www.nytimes.com/2011/02/01/health/research/01mcculloch.html.

2. Joe Sornberger, *Dreams & Due Diligence: Till and McCulloch's Stem Cell Discovery and Legacy* (Toronto, Canada: University of Toronto Press, 2011), p. 23.
3. Alice Taylor, "This 'Bomber' Actually Saved Countless Lives: U of T Alumnus Harold Johns Pioneered a New Kind of Cancer Treatment Dubbed the 'Cobalt Bomb,'" *University of Toronto Magazine*, January 13, 2017, https://magazine.utoronto.ca/campus/history/this-bomber-actually-saved-countless-lives-harold-johns-cobalt-60-cancer-therapy/.
4. cdnmedhall, "Dr. James Till-Dr. Ernest McCulloch Canadian Medical Hall of Fame Laureate," YouTube, January 6, 2011, https://www.youtube.com/watch?v=P7N-fUKjT-s&feature=player_embedded.
5. cdnmedhall, "Dr. James Till-Dr. Ernest McCulloch."
6. Taylor.
7. cdnmedhall, "Dr. Harold Johns, The Canadian Medical Hall of Fame," YouTube, December 29, 2010, http://www.cdnmedhall.org/inductees/dr-harold-johns.
8. cdnmedhall, "Dr James Till-Dr. Ernest McCulloch."
9. Friends of CIHR, "Dr. Jim Till, 'The Theory Behind the Stem Cell Concept,' FCIHR Video History," YouTube, August 20, 2012, https://www.youtube.com/watch?v=7eUQO-WKykY.
10. Joe Sornberger, "T.O. Stem Cell Pioneers Win 'America's Nobel,'" *Toronto Star,* September 18, 2005.
11. Ernest A. McCulloch, *The Ontario Cancer Institute: Successes and Reverses at Sherbourne Street* (Montreal, Canada: McGill-Queen University Press, 2003), p. 19.

Chapter Three The Discovery

1. J. E. Till and E. A. McCulloch. "A Direct Measurement of the Radiation Sensitivity of Normal Mouse Bone Marrow Cells." *Radiation Research* 14, no. 2 (Feb. 1961): pp. 213–222, www.jstor.org/stable/3570892.

2. Till and McCulloch.
3. cdnmedhall, "Dr. James Till-Dr. Ernest McCulloch Canadian Medical Hall of Fame Laureate," YouTube, January 6, 2011, https://www.youtube.com/watch?v=P7N-fUKjT-s&feature =player_embedded.
4. Joe Sornberger, *Dreams & Due Diligence: Till and McCulloch's Stem Cell Discovery and Legacy* (Toronto, Canada: University of Toronto Press, 2011), p. 32.
5. Sornberger, p. 33.
6. Friends of CIHR, "Dr. Jim Till, 'The Theory Behind the Stem Cell Concept,' FCIHR Video History," YouTube, August 20, 2012, https://www.youtube.com/watch?v=7eUQO-WKykY.
7. Sornberger, p. 34.
8. "90th Anniversary Issue. The Space Race, Technological Optimism and Other Highlights, 1960–69," *Science News*, March 24, 2017, https://www.sciencenews.org/article/90th-anniversary-issue-1960s.
9. Ernest A. McCulloch, *The Ontario Cancer Institute: Successes and Reverses at Sherbourne Street* (Montreal, Canada: McGill-Queen University Press, 2003), p. 49.
10. "Stem Cells and Their Dual Properties: Self-Renewal And Differentiation," Lasker Foundation, 2005, http://www .laskerfoundation.org/awards/show/stem-cells-and-their -dual-properties-self-renewal-and-differentiation/#james-till.
11. Sornberger, p. 35.
12. "Stem Cells and Their Dual Properties."
13. Miguel Ramalho-Santos and Holger Willenbring, "On the Origin of the Term Stem Cell," *Cell Stem Cell* 1, no. 1 (June 7, 2007): pp. 35–38, DOI:https://doi.org/10.1016/j. stem.2007.05.013.
14. Ramalho-Santos and Willenbring, p. 36.
15. Bob McDonald, "James Till and Ernest McCulloch, Stem Cell Researchers," *Quirks and Quarks*, October 29, 2005,

https://www.cbc.ca/archives/entry/james-till-and-ernest
-mcculloch-stem-cell-researchers.

16. McCulloch, p. 55.
17. Sornberger, p. 36.

Chapter Four ⚛ A Quiet Victory

1. Joe Sornberger, "T.O. Stem Cell Pioneers Win 'America's Nobel,'" *Toronto Star,* September 18, 2005.
2. Lawrence K. Altman, "5 Pioneers Are Awarded Lasker Medical Prizes," *New York Times*, September 18, 2005, https://www.nytimes.com/2005/09/18/science/five-pioneers -are-awarded-lasker-medical-prizes.html.
3. Saul J. Sharkis, "Canadian Stem Cell Scientists Take the Prize," *Cell* 122, no. 6 (September 23, 2005), https://www .cell.com/cell/fulltext/S0092-8674(05)00919-0.
4. Sornberger.
5. Altman.
6. E. A. McCulloch and J. E Till, "Perspectives on the Properties of Stem Cells," *Nature Medicine* 11, no. 10 (October 2005), http://go.galegroup.com/ps/i.do?p=SCIC&u=dclib_ain&id= GALE|A192625764&v=2.1&it=r&sid=SCIC&asid=- c30a4e47.
7. cdnmedhall, "Dr. James Till-Dr. Ernest McCulloch Canadian Medical Hall of Fame Laureate," YouTube, January 6, 2011, https://www.youtube.com/watch?v=P7N-fUKjT-s&feature =player_embedded.
8. "Dr. Ernest McCulloch," Canadian Medical Hall of Fame, http://www.cdnmedhall.org/inductees/dr-ernest-mcculloch (accessed April 15, 2019).
9. "Stem Cells and Their Dual Properties: Self-Renewal And Differentiation," Lasker Foundation, 2005, http://www.lasker foundation.org/awards/show/stem-cells-and-their-dual -properties-self-renewal-and-differentiation/#james-till.

10. Joe Sornberger, *Dreams & Due Diligence: Till and McCulloch's Stem Cell Discovery and Legacy* (Toronto, Canada: University of Toronto Press, 2011), p. 129.

Chapter Five 🔅 Moving Forward

1. Joe Sornberger, *Dreams & Due Diligence: Till and McCulloch's Stem Cell Discovery and Legacy* (Toronto, Canada: University of Toronto Press, 2011), p. 42.
2. Ernest A McCulloch, *The Ontario Cancer Institute: Successes and Reverses at Sherbourne Street* (Montreal, Canada: McGill-Queen University Press, 2003), p. 118.
3. Denise Gellene, "E. Donnall Thomas, Who Advanced Bone Marrow Transplants, Dies at 92," *New York Times*, October 22, 2012, https://www.nytimes.com/2012/10/22/science/e-donnall-thomas-furthered-bone-marrow-transplants-dies.html.
4. "Fathers of the Field: How Two Quiet Canadians Changed the Course of History in Biological Research," *Stem Cell Network* 5, no. 1 (Summer 2006), http://wwwstudies.uhn research.ca/stemspec/pdf/Summer06_SCN.pdf.
5. Effimia Christidi, "An Interview with Dr. Connie Eaves," BCREGMED Newsletter, December 14, 2018, https://bcreg med.ca/an-interview-with-dr-connie-eaves/.
6. "Fathers of the Field."
7. cdnmedhall, "Dr. Louis Siminovitch," YouTube, January 11, 2010, https://www.youtube.com/watch?v=izukkcPGLEY.
8. cdnmedhall.
9. Christidi.
10. "Fathers of the Field."

Chapter Six 🔅 What's Next for Stem Cells

1. Susannah Locke, "Stem Cells Were One of the Biggest Controversies of 2001. Where Are They Now?" *Vox*,

December 15, 2014, https://www.vox.com/2014/12/15/7384457/stem-cell.
2. Locke.
3. "Stem Cell Basics IV," National Institutes of Health, https://stemcells.nih.gov/info/basics/4.htm (accessed April 15, 2019).
4. Anna MacDonald, "Stem Cells in Drug Discovery," *Technology Networks*, April 4, 2017, https://www.technologynetworks.com/cell-science/articles/stem-cells-in-drug-discovery-286825.
5. "Types of Stem Cell Transplants for Cancer Treatment," American Cancer Society, https://www.cancer.org/treatment/treatments-and-side-effects/treatment-types/stem-cell-transplant/types-of-transplants.html (accessed April 15, 2019).
6. "Stem Cell Basics IV."
7. M. A. Borisov et al., "Stem Cells in the Treatment of Insulin-Dependent Diabetes Mellitus," *Acta Naturae* 8, no. 3 (July–September 2016): pp. 31–43, https://www.ncbi.nlm.nih.gov/pubmed/27795842.

Conclusion

1. Bob McDonald, "James Till and Ernest McCulloch, Stem Cell Researchers," *Quirks and Quarks,* October 29, 2005, https://www.cbc.ca/archives/entry/james-till-and-ernest-mcculloch-stem-cell-researchers.
2. cdnmedhall, "Dr. James Till-Dr. Ernest McCulloch Canadian Medical Hall of Fame Laureate," YouTube, January 6, 2011, https://www.youtube.com/watch?v=P7N-fUKjT-s&t=5s.

GLOSSARY

bone marrow A substance found within bones that produces blood cells.

chromosome A small X-shaped structure inside a cell that contains genes.

collaborate To work together on a project.

embryo An animal or plant in the early developmental stages, from the first cell division after egg fertilization.

fertilize To form a zygote by combining a sperm and an egg.

hematopoietic stem cell A cell that can develop into different types of blood cells, such as red blood cells, white blood cells, and platelets.

leukemia A cancer of the blood, often characterized by an increase in white blood cells.

peer-reviewed journal A magazine or periodical with articles checked by fellow scientists before being published.

prostate A male reproductive gland located below the bladder.

serendipity The phenomenon of a positive event happening completely by chance.

spleen An organ in the abdomen responsible for red blood cell recycling and antibody and certain white blood cell creation.

stem cell An unspecialized cell with the ability to replicate and to develop into a specific cell type.

transplant To transfer biological material (usually organ or tissues) from one person to another.

FURTHER READING

BOOKS

Borus, Audrey. *James Watson, Francis Crick, Rosalind Franklin, and Maurice Wilkins: The Scientists Who Revealed the Structure of DNA*. New York, NY: Enslow Publishing, 2020.

Eaton, Louise, and Kara Rogers. *Examining Cells*. New York, NY: Britannica Educational Publishing in association with Rosen Educational Services, 2018.

Edwards, Sue B. *Stem Cells*. Lake Elmo, MN: Focus Readers, 2019.

Jackson, Tom. *Is Human Cloning in Our Future? Theories About Genetics*. New York, NY: Gareth Stevens Publishing, 2019.

Rauf, Don. *Inheritance and Variation of Traits*. New York, NY: Enslow Publishing, 2018.

WEBSITES

A Closer Look at Stem Cells
www.closerlookatstemcells.org
Read more about stem cells and their applications in medicine.

American Museum of Natural History: The Gene Scene
www.amnh.org/explore/ology/genetics
Learn all about genetics with experiments, videos, games, and more from the American Museum of Natural History.

National Institutes of Health: A Revolution in Progress: Human Genetics and Medical Research
history.nih.gov/exhibits/genetics
Dive deeper into genetics, including gene therapy, the human genome project, and ethics.

INDEX